DOGGLEBOX

CHARLIE ELLIS

WHAT DOGS REALLY THINK ABOUT TELEVISION

summersdale

DOGGLEBOX

Summersdale Publishers Ltd
46 West Street
Chichester
West Sussex
PO19 1RP
UK

www.summersdale.com

Printed and bound in the Czech Republic

ISBN: 978-1-84953-994-4

Substantial discounts on bulk quantities of Summersdale books are available to corporations, professional associations and other organisations. For details contact Nicky Douglas by telephone: +44 (0) 1243 756902, fax: +44 (0) 1243 786300 or email: nicky@summersdale.com.

Dogs may be man's best friends, but all those years spent snuggling with us on the sofa have taught them more than just how to locate the comfiest spot – they've also become avid telly watchers, with a nose for a good show. You may think your pooches spend all day waiting for you to come home, but the truth is that they've been soaking up soap operas and binging on boxsets while you were out.

It's time to lean back, put your feet up and join the nation's most lovable TV critics, as you enter the wonderful world of *Dogglebox*!

WHY ARE THERE SO MANY ADVERTS FOR ANTI-WRINKLE CREAM? I THOUGHT MY WRINKLES WERE CUTE!

I COULD BE ON
TODDLERS & TIARAS –
I LIKE SPARKLY THINGS,
I WEAR CUTE BOWS AND
YES, I SUPPOSE I *AM*
A BIT OF A DIVA.

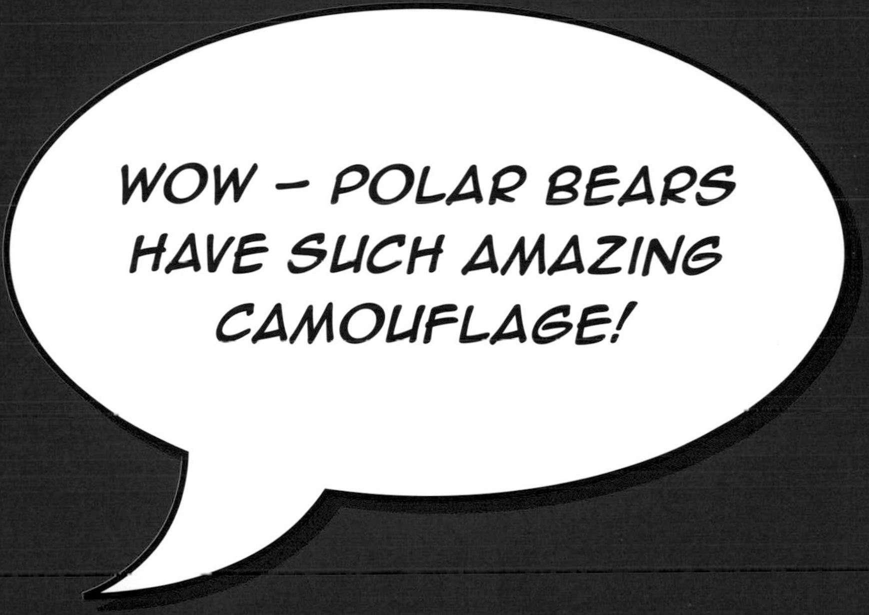
WOW – POLAR BEARS HAVE SUCH AMAZING CAMOUFLAGE!

PIPPA, COULD YOU *PLEASE* STOP ARGUING WITH YOUR BROTHER FOR JUST FIVE MINUTES WHILE I WATCH MY PROGRAMME?

YEAH, IT'S A NICE HOUSE, KIRSTIE, BUT WHAT ABOUT THE LOCAL WALKS?!

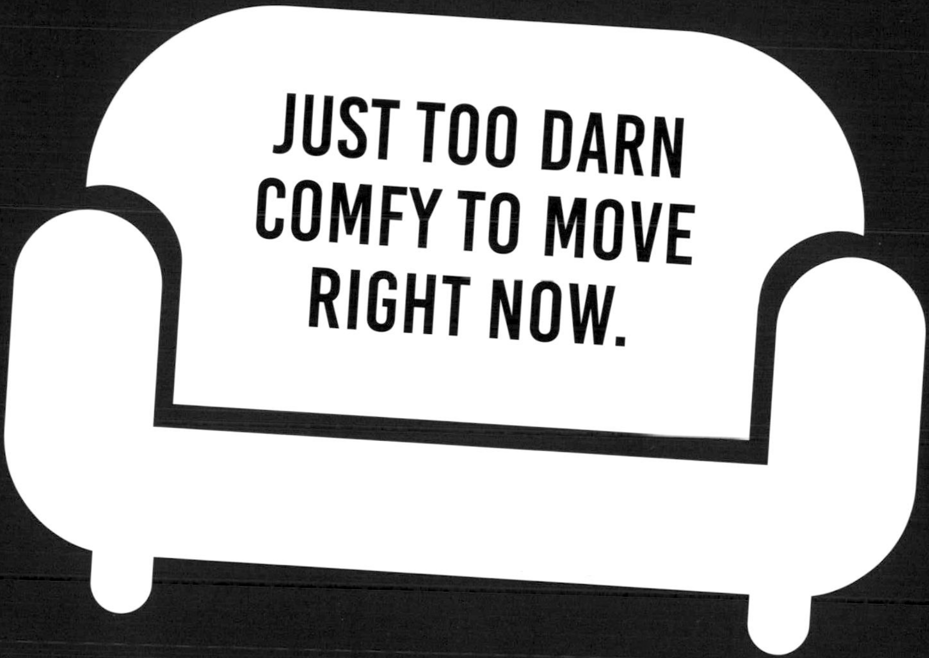
JUST TOO DARN
COMFY TO MOVE
RIGHT NOW.

GOODNESS ME, SHE PUT *FAR* TOO MUCH SALT IN THE SAUCE. I DON'T THINK SHE'LL MAKE IT TO THE FINAL NOW.

YOU WANT TO GO FOR A WALK NOW? BUT MISS MARPLE IS ABOUT TO REVEAL WHO THE MURDERER IS!

THIS *SEWING BEE* LARK IS A LOT MORE DIFFICULT THAN IT LOOKS – ESPECIALLY WITHOUT THUMBS!

IF I STARE AT THE TV LONG ENOUGH, I'M SURE I CAN SUMMON THAT JUICY STEAK OUT OF THE SCREEN...

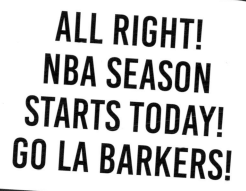

HEADLOCK! TAP OUT WHILE YOU STILL CAN.
I'M NEVER WATCHING THE WRESTLING WITH YOU AGAIN.

MY FAVOURITE COMFORT VIEWING: *THE GREAT BRITISH BARK OFF*.

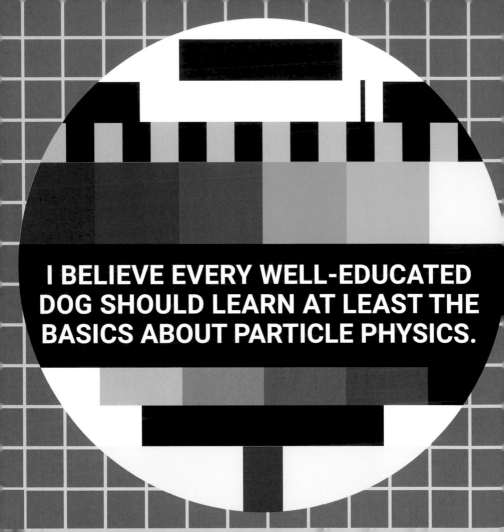

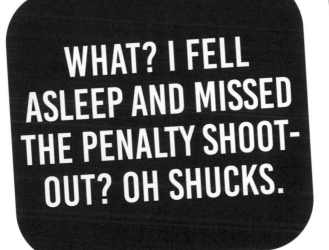

HOW IS FLYNN RIDER EVER GOING TO SAVE ME FROM MY TOWER IF I DON'T HAVE LONG HAIR – OR AT LEAST LONGER EARS?

IT'S IMPORTANT TO TAKE REGULAR BREAKS WHEN DOING THE HOUSEWORK. AND BESIDES, IT'S NEARLY TIME FOR *LOOSE WOMEN*!

BUT THE DOCTOR AND ROSE WERE MEANT TO BE TOGETHER FOREVER...

OH, *TOP GEAR* JUST ISN'T THE SAME ANY MORE...

WELL, EVEN FROM THIS ANGLE THAT WEDDING CAKE LOOKS WONKY. WHATEVER WILL THE BRIDE SAY?

I'M JUST GOING UNDER MY BLANKET – WILL YOU TELL ME WHEN THE SCARY BIT ENDS, PLEASE?

NOW I CAN FINALLY WATCH *NEIGHBOURS* THE WAY THEY DO IN AUSTRALIA.

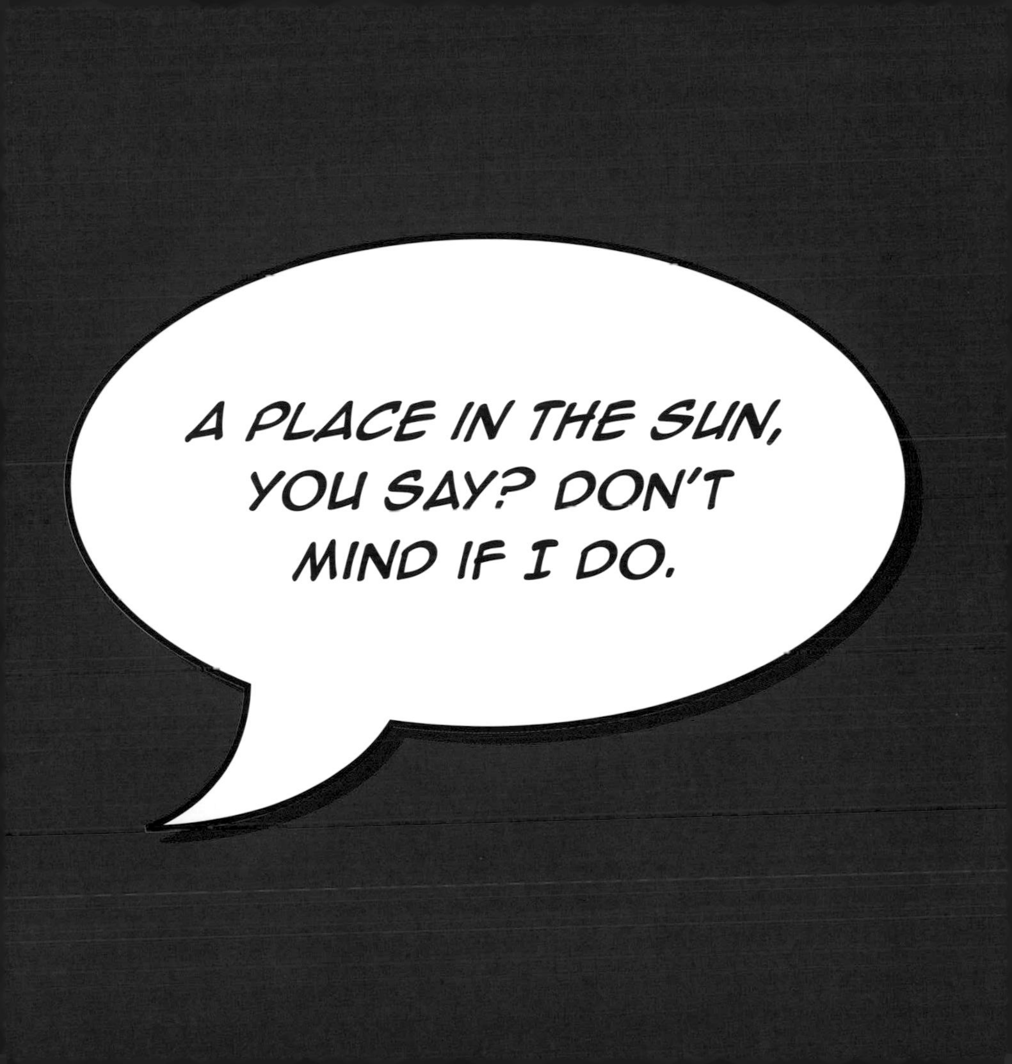
A PLACE IN THE SUN, YOU SAY? DON'T MIND IF I DO.

SO IF HE'S KEYSER SÖZE, THEN WHO'S...? AND WHAT DID...? AND WHY...? HUMPH, I DON'T GET IT!

HANG ON, IS ORANGE THE NEW BLACK, OR IS BLACK THE NEW BLACK NOW?

PHOTO CREDITS

If you're interested in finding out more about our books, find us on Facebook at **Summersdale Publishers** and follow us on Twitter at **@Summersdale**.

www.summersdale.com